Matteo Carbone
Andrea Silvello

All the Insurance Players Will Be Insurtech

Matteo Carbone
Andrea Silvello

All the Insurance Players Will Be Insurtech

A wave of innovation is finally reshaping the insurance industry

Scholars' Press

Imprint
Any brand names and product names mentioned in this book are subject to trademark, brand or patent protection and are trademarks or registered trademarks of their respective holders. The use of brand names, product names, common names, trade names, product descriptions etc. even without a particular marking in this work is in no way to be construed to mean that such names may be regarded as unrestricted in respect of trademark and brand protection legislation and could thus be used by anyone.

Cover image: www.ingimage.com

Publisher:
Scholars' Press
is a trademark of
International Book Market Service Ltd., member of OmniScriptum Publishing Group
17 Meldrum Street, Beau Bassin 71504, Mauritius

Printed at: see last page
ISBN: 978-620-2-30419-1

Copyright © Matteo Carbone, Andrea Silvello
Copyright © 2017 International Book Market Service Ltd., member of OmniScriptum Publishing Group
All rights reserved. Beau Bassin 2017

Contents

Introduction

The digital revolution is happening now……………………………......................3

Chapter 1

A deep evolution of the insurance industry…………………………………………..5

Chapter 2

How to innovate and maximize the opportunity: the CPs of InsurTech………….15

Chapter 3

The world will be connected, but the risks and intermediaries are here to stay….22

Chapter 4

The three pillars of connected insurance: motor, home and health……………......30

Chapter 5

Micro insurance: engaging customers in the right way, at the right time………....54

Chapter 6

Our InsurTech predictions... 40

References…………………………………………………………………....... 59

The digital revolution is happening now

Imagine having an insurance "agent" on your smart phone, in a single app. With just a tap or two, you can insure anything you own at any time, for as long or as little as you like.

Your insurance app, which has been paying attention to your wants and needs, makes suggestions from time to time—suggesting travel insurance after you've booked a flight, and, when you move into a new apartment, prompting you to update your renter's insurance. What's more, the packages you see fit your budget. *That's* service!

The digital revolution is happening now, transforming the way we live, work, play, and shop, and empowering customers as never before. Already we see these changes in retail, travel, fashion, and other mature businesses. It's happening in industries, too, such as e-commerce, with its customized offers tailored to individual wants, needs, and habits. Ultimately, it will disrupt even those sectors resistant to change. Even banking sector, notoriously conservative, is embracing technology. Can the staid insurance industry be far behind?

The change is inevitable, and filled with promise. Soon, our lifestyles will influence the price of health or risk coverage we buy, rewarding good behaviors such as daily exercise and healthy eating habits. Good drivers will pay less for auto insurance.

As insurance technology becomes the rule, insurance's role will expand, too, to include risk prevention and management. Imagine that you have a car accident and the "black box" provided by your insurer calls the ambulance and saves your life. Imagine landing in a foreign airport and getting an invitation on your phone to insure your stay for the time you are there or, just after you make plans to play football with your friends, you receive a notification inviting you to cover the risk of injuries during the game.

Can you imagine these scenarios? Many are doing so, and taking steps to turn these visions into reality. Insurance technology, or InsurTech, is a rapidly growing niche, its innovators poised to disrupt the insurance industry. This is already happening, in fact, as new, mobile-friendly, customer-centric startups begin snapping up market share with apps that make insurance easy and even enjoyable to buy and manage.

The InsurTech train is leaving the station. Traditional insurance companies, or "incumbents," who cling to the old ways may miss it entirely, and be left behind. Already we are seeing an exciting new roster of InsurTech players emerging with innovative, exciting solutions to longstanding insurance problems. More competitors are on their way, and the ride promises to be exhilarating. When it takes off, will you be on board?

—Andrea Silvello and Matteo Carbone

1

A deep evolution of the insurance industry

Every insurance player will be InsurTech

Before we begin our journey, let us look to where we have been—as far back as 640 years ago, when insurance began providing protection for people in life and in employment. Since 1347—the year of the first known insurance contract, in Genoa, Italy—people have drawn up contracts in which someone promises to indemnify another against loss or damage from an uncertain event, so long as a premium is paid to obtain this coverage.

This model has remained largely unaltered over the years. With such a long history, is it any wonder that the industry has been slow to change? People and businesses still buy insurance using these time-tested models, and studies show that consumer confidence in the industry is high. Why fix a system that isn't broken?

On the other hand, the way insurance works—or doesn't work—for consumers is deeply flawed. Customers often have difficulty understanding what their policies offer because of complicated contracts that are difficult to follow. And with "one-size-fits-all" templates predominating, many are realizing that the quotes they receive do not reflect their individual needs or situations.

More than any other traits, rigidity and complexity are most often associated with insurance coverage and insurers. The insurance field, in other words, is wide open for disruption. And consumers are now demanding it.

What has made the difference? Technology. Digital, especially mobile, has enabled industries including retail, banking, and travel to offer their customers ease of use, transparency, and accessibility—features we now expect from all the businesses and services we use. Today's insurance customers want coverage tailored to their needs, and will choose value over price. They also expect their insurers to provide easy access to information via whatever channel the customer prefers.

If traditional insurance providers are slow to react to this new, "customer-centric" environment, newcomers are poised to fill the gaps. Already insurance technology startups are beginning to render old, standardized models obsolete—by shifting their focus toward context and utility, and presenting customized choices tailored to individual needs. In this new way of doing insurance, customers get personalized offers delivered at the right time, in the right way, and at the right price.

Good news for insurers

Fortunately, what is good for customers is great for insurance providers—assuming they adapt to the times by innovating and adopting these new technologies. Pleasing customers ought to be a prime motivator in itself, but insurers who truly embrace digital will find their business improved in ways they had not imagined: streamlined processes, enhanced efficiency, lowered risk, and diminished loss ratios.

This is great news for the insurance industry. Despite dire warnings that our sector is becoming obsolete, we are convinced that insurance companies will still be relevant in the future, or will become even more relevant than they are now. Those that succeed, however, will be not just insurance players but InsurTechs, using technology as the main enabler for reaching their strategic objectives.

InsurTechs have great potential to disrupt the industry. Traditional insurers still make the rules because they possess the capital, infrastructure, and institutional knowledge, but they will lose the upper hand unless they embrace the solutions put forward by InsurTech startups – which are legacy-system free, resourceful, and creative, but usually lack in-depth knowledge about the insurance sector.

To remain relevant, insurance companies must themselves become InsurTechs. But how, when they lack technological know-how? One answer is to work hand-in-hand with the newcomers, entering into a deep collaboration to deliver innovative solutions. Many experienced professionals have predicted these types of partnerships, and we are already seeing some great examples.

The reach of this digital transformation goes way beyond the elimination of the "middle man" or changes in distribution methods.

In fact, the direct digital channel, in which all transactions are digital, dominates very few markets, and usually deals only with compulsory insurance. In most markets, multi-channel prevails, and customers choose—with variations from country to country—to interact with an intermediary at some point.

Even so, technology is revolutionizing the way we do insurance, from underwriting to claims, and beyond.

How to get there

Every insurance sector player—whether it's a reinsurer, a carrier or an intermediary—ought to consider this question: How should the insurance value chain be reshaped using the new technologies at hand? As of this writing, technologies include the cloud, the Internet of Things (IoT), big data and advanced analytics, quantum computing, artificial intelligence, autonomous agents, drones, blockchain, virtual reality, and self-driving cars.

To take full advantage of these technologies, the insurance professional must:
1. Identify use cases that contribute to reaching strategic business goals,
2. Apply these examples to maximize the effects of each player inside the insurance value chain, and
3. Consider the software/hardware selection or "make vs. buy" choices.

In today's insurance arena, there is no such thing as "one size fits all." Each player needs to create customized use cases based on their individual strategy and characteristics.

If this sounds daunting, take heart: you are not alone. The insurance sector is undergoing a profound change. Digital transformation has become a major challenge for insurance companies all over the world.

Use cases: insurance IoT

In Italy, the extent and popularity of this shift can be seen in the adoption of vehicle telematics, also known as Usage-Based Insurance, which uses technology to track and report driver behaviors and vehicle use, enabling insurers to adjust premiums accordingly.

According to the latest IVASS data, almost 20 percent of new policies and renewals in Italy included the use of "black boxes" in motor vehicles. That's a good chunk of the market, and the number rises each year. More than 70 percent of Italians responding to an SSI survey expressed a positive attitude toward motor telematics insurance, indicating widespread acceptance.

Italy has long been known as a frontrunner in insurance innovation. How is the technology faring elsewhere? At the end of 2015, half the 10 million connected cars in the world had a telematics insurance policy.

Telematics offers many benefits, including reduced premiums for drivers. Insurers benefit from having more data to help them fine-tune their policies and products, and may even see their loss ratios improve. According to an Insurance Research Council survey, 56 of drivers polled said the use of telematics had made them better drivers.

Connected to the Internet and providing driver data to insurers, telematics is one example of how the IoT may drive the "connected insurance" phenomenon. The Internet of Things comprises a network or system of interrelated computing devices and sensors communicating with one another. These objects, or "things," can transmit data.

The insurance industry has always been rich in data but, traditionally, that data is unstructured, or the models used are old and simple. Data analytics can structure this information in new ways so that it answers specific questions—about how a person drives, for instance, or how much they exercise. The exciting implications of this technology has made being "connected" the talk of the town, including among insurers who embrace change and innovation.

Consumers are becoming more and more "connected," at home, at work, behind the wheel, when they engage in sports and leisure activities, and so on. The surrounding "smart" environment is part of a larger connected "ecosystem," creating new opportunities for insurance companies.

To get the most value from this ecosystem, insurers must manage its components properly: sensors, computers, wearables, and data. Again, big data analytics plays a huge role, as the quantity of collected data and variables continues to grow. IoT's real-time data collection and sharing power will create significant new opportunities: finer product segmentation plus more specialized risk pools and predictive modeling to better assess that risk, improve loss control, and accelerate premium growth.

To harness the power of the IoT, insurance carriers will need to think creatively about which data to gather and how to use it. A system based on IoT and big data analytics that can identify patterns and provide optimized solutions based on real-time input, up-front, may result in a seamless, user-friendly interface that will transform the way companies communicate with policy holders.

IoT's impact within insurance is coming fully into focus. At the highest level, better use of IoT and sensor data means insurers have the opportunity to:

- Establish direct, unmediated customer relationships,
- Gain a more granular, precise understanding of who their customers are and how their needs change over time, and
- Individualize offerings of products and features.

The rise of the bot: insurance AI

Within IoT applications, artificial intelligence (AI) is also helping the sector (or disrupting it, depending on your point of view). AI offers predictive recommendations backed by complex algorithms and data, and can analyze process flows for bottlenecks, improving overall company and customer satisfaction.

Algorithms compare answers and information provided by customers to make appropriate recommendations for each risk scenario.

Via machine learning, AI works continually to better understand humans and their thought processes, analyze human behavior, and provide predictive consulting based on each individual's wants and needs.

In spite of these advantages and more, incumbent insurance players have been slow to adopt digital strategies. To survive, they will need to change their mindsets soon, and very quickly.

A host of digital start-ups has already entered the field and many others are poised on the horizon to compete with traditionals for business, especially from millennial consumers and "Gen C" (for "Connected"). These newcomers, called "InsurTechs," have already begun to shake up the industry. Many see them as a fresh alternative to the incumbent's model of doing business in today's and tomorrow's connected world.

How we benefit

We have identified four main benefits that "connected insurance" provides to the insurance sector:

1. **A bolstered bottom line**, creating value by improving insurance profit-and-loss, and sharing this value with the customer;
2. **Enhanced proximity and interactions** with the customer, as well as new customer experiences and services;
3. **Knowledge creation and consolidation,** as data provides more information about risks and the customer base, and
4. **Sustainability,** not only for the insurer, but for society as a whole.

A new frontier: 'Push' mobile micro insurance

Mandatory insurance, sought by the customer who must get coverage or suffer consequences, represents the bulk of policies sold. People are much less interested in, and receptive to, non-compulsory insurance—which makes it a market ripe for the plucking. As we say in the insurance industry: "Insurance is sold, not bought," and "the only thing more difficult to sell than insurance is non-compulsory insurance." Technology can change this paradigm.

Even as smart phones become more and more integral to customers' daily lives, however, most insurers seem unable or unwilling to make use of mobile technologies to fill the non-compulsory gap. InsurTechs have no such qualms.

Micro-insurance holds great potential for revolutionizing the insurance sales process. It also may help reduce the protection gap in developed countries for several types of risks, and it can be a way to target millennials who have limited financial resources and low trust in traditional intermediaries.

The main function of micro-insurance is to deliver innovation to customers who seek it. At the same time, it helps insurers gain insights into individual clients, helping them to anticipate and address customers' needs without second-guessing.

Micro-insurance can also be considered a form of micro-financing, because it offers low-cost coverage of specific risks for specific durations. Its applications could be huge, encompassing data and data analytics to add value for insurers and customers. It will almost certainly attract major investors. As a tool to provide custom, niche products in the sharing economy, micro-insurance holds the power to take insurance to the next level in our new, customer-centric world.

Characteristics of an insurable risk		Instant push insurance
1. Need	Need for insurance cover when the anticipated event occurs	✓ Use cases that target specific needs
2. Mutuality	Large number of similar exposure units	✓ Need to build vast user base
3. Randomness	Accidental and unintentional loss	✓ Push approach to limit adverse selection
4. Assessability	The peril must be assessable in terms of possible losses and determinable if the loss is covered by the policy	✓ Use cases designed to cover specific risks that are easy to identify and to communicate
5. Economic viability	No catastrophic loss exposure for the insurer	✓ Use cases which avoid the accumulation of exposure to catastrophic risks
6. Affordability	The premium level considering administrative and distribution costs have to be sustainable by the insured	✓ Use cases with limited expected frequency or automatic claims (ex. flight delay)

Image 1. *Characteristics of an insurable risk vs. instant push insurance*

"Push" mobile micro-insurance, in which suggestions for purchases appear on the consumer's phone at appropriate times, is the latest, greatest example so far of how technology can revitalize the insurance industry.

In the Italian InsurTech start-up Neosurance we see the first worldwide example of push micro-insurance with a B2B2C business model. In push mobile micro-insurance, InsurTechs may find a solution to the anti-selection issue that troubles the on-demand insurance space. This new approach to selling insurance addresses existing challenges by using digital (mobile) channels for communication, registration, payment of premiums and claims processing (submissions and payouts).

Most customers are not only under-insured, but also unaware of their potential needs for coverage. In the most advanced micro-insurance apps, an artificial insurance agent, like a knowledgeable, capable human, motivates the customer to buy protection by offering the right coverage at the right time on the customer's smart phone, stimulating impulse purchases of small-ticket insurance.

The smart phone is no longer just a channel, but, now, a proxy of the customer. Just as an agent knows its client, AI learns and gathers in-depth knowledge about the customer by analyzing behaviors, context and even emotions—all channeled through the smart phone. In this way, technology can create a continuous cycle of insight-driven and highly personalized contextual interactions.

Every successful insurer will be InsurTech

In this age of the "fourth industrial revolution," risks are changing. The advent of technology has made digital assets more valuable than physical ones. Against this scenario, the insurance sector must deal with technological change and disruption, and reconsider the way it defines itself. InsurTech is helping to redefine the way the insurance industry is perceived.

It's unthinkable for an insurer today not to ask how to evolve business architecture by considering which modules within their value chain they should transform or reinvent using technology and data.

We believe all the players in the insurance arena will be InsurTech—that is, organizations where technology will prevail as the key enabler for the achievement of their strategic goals.

InsurTech start-ups have received almost than $20 billion in funding to date. Fantastic teams and interesting new insurance cases have been grabbing the attention of analysts.

Full-stack insurtech start-ups are generating a lot of excitement in the investor community and attracting relevant funds, and some have achieved stellar valuations, with Oscar, Lemonade, Sonnet, Root, Alan, Element, and Zhong An some of the most fascinating players.

An increasingly popular business model is the MGA/MGU approach (Managing General Agents/Managing General Underwriter), a way to satisfy investors' appetite for players covering a large number of the activities in the insurance value chain, and for partnering with incumbents only for underwriting. Examples include Trov, Slice, so-sure, Insure The Box, Bought By Many, and Prima.

Incumbents can innovate, and incumbents and InsurTech startups can, and should, collaborate. Consider, for example, the impressive international success of players such as the digital insurance platform Guidewire and Octo Telematics. We believe service providers for the insurance sector will be more successful in scaling to an international level than the other models described above. This kind of collaboration makes use of incumbents' technical knowledge and their customers' trust. Especially promising are partnerships between incumbents and specialized tech startups providing them with innovative ways of doing business.

As we embark on this transformative, collaborative journey, let us keep in mind three lessons we in Italy learned from the success of connected car insurance:

- **Transformation does not happen overnight.** Telematics needed years of experimentation before becoming pervasive among big Italian companies, followed by a "me, too" approach from competitors, and a number of use cases, to reach its current adoption growth.
- **Companies can lead this transformation.** The black-box data that telematics provides can enable insurers to offer more and better services to customers— something they want. According to recent international studies, clients are requesting that their policies be integrated with service platforms. These studies also show that people trust their insurance companies, which makes service providers want to partner with them.
- **If insurance companies do not take advantage of this opportunity, some other player will.** Metromile, an InsurTech startup and digital distributor, has created a telematics auto insurance policy with an insurance company playing the role of underwriter. After acquiring nearly $200 million in funding, Metromile in 2016 bought Mosaic Insurance, becoming the first InsurTech startup to buy a traditional insurance company. Software is, indeed, "eating the world"— even in the insurance sector.

2

How to innovate and maximize the opportunity

The 'CPs' of connected insurance

In today's fast-changing world, "innovate-or-die" has become not only a business mantra, but a given. By placing a world of choices in our hands, technology has empowered the consumer as never before. Any enterprise that does not adopt a "customer-centric" focus will lose business to others who are more than willing to take up the slack.

The insurance industry is no exception to this rule. And, although the sector is commonly perceived as slow-changing, it has actually shown quite a capacity for innovation.

Digital insurance distribution, for example, began as far back as the early 1980s, when the German Post Office experimented with remote insurance sales in Berlin and Düsseldorf using *Bildschirmtext*—data transmitted through the telephone network and displayed on a television set. Today, UK consumers buy nearly 60 percent of their auto insurance online, and consumers commonly use comparison websites when purchasing auto insurance. Few other industries have embraced digital distribution so widely or so well.

Health insurance, too, offers many examples of innovations that use technology.

In the last twenty years, the South African insurer Discovery has introduced a number of ways to improve policyholders' lives using connected fitness devices: tracking healthy behaviors, generating discounts, and providing incentives for activities supporting wellness and even healthy food purchases. Discovery has replicated its "Vitality" model in different locales and business lines, and has motivated its customers to continually increase the number of connected devices they use to provide data to the company. The insurer has even extended its incentives to other insurance lines: Vitalitydrive rewards drivers for their driving knowledge, course attendance, and good driving behaviors with discounts of up to 50 percent on fuel purchases.

Innovation is accelerating in the industry, too. New and emerging technologies are providing user experiences much different from the confusing, complex enrollment and claims processes for which insurance providers have become infamous. Institutions with hundreds of years of tradition are rethinking their insurance business models and identifying areas in their own value chain to transform or reinvent with the help of technology.

Hardly a day goes by, it seems, without some new insurance application or service appearing on the scene. Broadly speaking, these innovations can be categorized according to seven macro areas:

- **Awareness:** generates awareness in the client of the need to be insured, and other marketing aspects of the specific brand/offer;
- **Choice:** offers an insurance value proposition, divided into two main groups:
    - **Aggregators** that compare different solutions, and
    - **Underwriters**, innovating ways to construct the offer for the specific client;
- **Purchase:** innovative ways to improve the act of selling, including the collection of premiums;
- **Use:** includes three very distinct steps of the insurance value chain, namely, policy handling, service delivery—which is becoming more and more important—and claims management;
- **Recommendation:** recommends purchases based on user data and experiences;
- **The Internet of Things (IoT),** the hardware and software solutions involved in "connected" insurance (such as motor insurance telematics), and
- **Peer to peer (P2P):** bringing *peer-to-peer* logic to the insurance environment, in a manner similar to the old mutual insurance model.

One of the main challenges for analysts, incumbents, startups, and investors is determining how relevant these innovations might be for the insurance sector. To succeed, which qualities or criteria should InsurTech startups meet? Taking a cue from the legal profession's "CPs," or "Conditions Precedent" that must be fulfilled to execute a commercial contract, we offer here our own CPs for InsurTech startups—conditions that must be met for success today.

Mind your Cs and Ps

First, let us consider the "5Cs" offered by Schwetak Verma, director of the MetLife Innovation Center in Singapore.

"I have interacted with various startups, and it has become clear that the breadth and scale of the opportunity are not clear to many of them," Verma says. "The mental model of InsurTech seems to be limited to the claims part of the value chain only."

Verma designed his framework to help startups devise a strategy for selling to insurance carriers. The 5Cs are:

- **Communication**: At its core, insurance is a promise. A promise holds little value if you can't communicate it.
- **Customization**: Verma sees two opportunities here: startups building recommendation engines to customize risk coverage, and those generating data sets that can be used to change the basis of underwriting. Tomorrow's leading carriers will embrace "real-time underwriting," he predicts, as customers produce more captureable data.
- **Connection**: Getting noticed is the key challenge. To stand out in the crowd, you must participate in your customers' conversations, engaging without interrupting. Many customers feel no true connection with, or loyalty to, their insurer, and insurance ranks near the bottom in customer

satisfaction. Ancillary digital services can help change that paradigm by offering more opportunities to connect with our customers.

- **Cognition**, including artificial intelligence (AI) and machine learning (ML). We are in the early stages of an AI revolution. In insurance, Verma sees AI/ML tools being used for:
    - Fraud detection and monitoring
    - Claims automation
    - Marketing, with customization
    - Behavioral analysis (for improved pricing)
    - Preventive insurance, using genomic data sets.
- **Consensus**, or blockchain. "Consensus" refers to the underlying algorithm that underpins blockchain's structure. Blockchain can have an enormous effect on administrative costs by increasing the ease and efficiency of processes such as Know Your Customer, fraud detection, and other verification services such as policy issue and claim filing. Ideally, the entire industry would collaborate on a blockchain solution.

Having advised nearly one hundred insurers, reinsurers, tech players and investors, we have formulated a set of criteria for determining the potential of each InsurTech initiative, whether executed by a startup or an incumbent. We've based our "Four Ps" on four fundamentals of the insurance business:

- **Profitability**: What effect might an innovation have on the profitability of the insurance portfolio, acting on the loss-ratio or cost level without an increase in volumes?
- **Proximity**: Does it have numerous touch points for improving the relationship with the customer?
- **Persistence**: Does it reach out effectively to increase renewal rates, thereby stabilizing the insurance portfolio?

- **Productivity**: How does it contribute at the top-line insurance level to new client acquisition, cross-selling, or fees for added services?

InsurTech is taking off, there is no doubt, as our world becomes ever more connected and technology pervades all aspects of life. Investment in InsurTech initiatives boomed in 2015-2017.

Threat or opportunity?

While some incumbents feel threatened by the industry's move to InsurTech, others embrace the trend as an opportunity to improve their core business and even to invest, perhaps setting up an internal innovation team, or investing in startup accelerators/incubators or in startups themselves.

Innovative initiatives are rapidly proliferating for all phases of the customer journey and along all steps in the insurance value chain, making for a very crowded map.

Devising something truly new

Change in the sector has largely occurred on an incremental level, focused on improving existing products and services rather than inventing new ones, or on merely adjusting our business model. As a result, we may be missing opportunities for transformation.

Why, for instance, do we dedicate our resources to compensating for losses rather than preventing them? Previously, there may have been too many unknowns for us to proactively help our clients avoid losses (and protect our own balance sheets), but with data now so readily available, our ability to manage risk ought to move loss prevention to the top of the priority list.

Think of the savings we in the insurance sector could realize if we knew in advance what our customers' weaknesses were behind the wheel, and could help them improve.

Privacy may be an issue, of course. Not everyone wants their driving behaviors tracked or their location available at all times. Insurers can answer these concerns by making the technology voluntary, even desirable. Consumers motivated to use a technology will trade a measure of privacy for the privilege, as they already do while using social media, car- and ride-sharing platforms, and search engines. The self-quantification movement, or "Internet of Me," is growing, with people using devices to gain insights about their daily habits, health, and lives. Everything is all about the customer—satisfying their demands, expectations, and needs.

Disrupting the culture

Rather than wondering whether reliance on technology, especially mobile technology, is increasing—it is—or whether we should make better use of the public enthrallment with tech to satisfy customers and improve our own business case—we should—we ought each to be asking which technologies are right for us, and how best to implement and use them.

Incumbents and innovators alike who embrace, explore, and exploit technology will stand the best chance of thriving in the years ahead. The rest will fall away, as obsolete as dinosaurs for failing to adapt. For this reason, we maintain that *all players in the insurance sector will become InsurTech.*

Because of our industry's reluctance to change, some predict a bleak winter lies ahead for insurers. We, however, think this "weakness"—caution—may ultimately prove to be one of our greatest strengths.

Stepping carefully and deliberately through the technology landscape may help us to avoid the pitfalls, including data breaches, ransomware attacks, and resulting reputational loss that others have experienced.

Going slowly can be good. Erring on the side of caution may keep us on the right side.

Crossing the finish line with cell phones in one hand, sensors in the other, and our systems and networks intact, we surely will find that, as the fable teaches, "Slow and steady wins the race."

3

The world will be connected

But the risks and intermediaries are here to stay

The insurance sector has entered a phase of profound, widespread transformation, with change encompassing all phases of the insurance value chain from underwriting to claims. What role, if any, will agents play in the arena of tomorrow?

So far, the direct digital channel dominates very few markets, and deals only with compulsory insurance. For the most part, a multichannel-oriented customer continues—with variations from country to country—to choose at some point to interact with an intermediary. Every insurance sector player—whether it's a reinsurer, a carrier or an intermediary—ought to ask this question: How can I use technology to reshape the insurance value chain?

Numerous relevant technologies come to mind, including the cloud, IoT, big data and advanced analytics, quantum computing, AI, autonomous agents, drones, blockchain, virtual reality, and self-driving cars.

To take full advantage of these technologies, we must first identify use cases that can help us reach our own strategic business goals, then apply these examples for maximum effect inside the insurance value chain of each player. Finally, we should look at the software and hardware selection or the "make vs. buy" choices, keeping in mind that one size does not fit all.

Tech is the wave of the future in every industry, including insurance, and we would do well to prepare ourselves.

Resistance is futile, in our opinion, but it is also understandable, especially in such a longstanding industry as insurance. Some are reluctant to embrace these new technologies out of an attachment to "the way things have always been done"—but for others, the primary obstacle is fear.

As a growing number of apps and online services help consumers to easily and conveniently choose and purchase coverage, pay less in premiums, file claims, and more, some are predicting the demise of the "middleman," causing anxiety in the industry.

In our new, connected world, what will happen to traditional insurance business models and jobs? Will brokers and agents go the way of the dinosaur? Will insurance itself become irrelevant?

We are convinced that insurance companies will still be relevant in the future—perhaps even more so than now—but they will have to be InsurTechs: players who use technology as the main enablers for reaching their objectives.

When cars drive themselves

The insurance line most likely to experience disruption in the coming years is automotive—because driving itself is on the verge of transformation. Technology is on the fast-track to produce self-driving cars, raising myriad questions about how insurance will work, and who and what will be covered, and how.

Autonomous vehicle technology holds great promise for safer, more efficient travel. It also stands to trigger a tectonic shift in auto insurance.

Tesla, for example, saw crash rates fall a whopping 40 percent after the company installed its Autopilot self-driving technology in its vehicles. And in partnership with Tesloop, a small ride-sharing service using Tesla cars in Southern California, Farmers Insurance reportedly cut risk premiums by 25 percent. Tesla CEO Elon Musk told *Business Insider* that he wants to see insurance companies drop their prices as risk diminishes. But will these kinds of premium adjustments hurt the insurance industry?

The global accounting firm KPMG has predicted that, within twenty-five years, autonomous-vehicle technology could cause the personal auto insurance sector to shrink by 40 percent. The risk may shift from drivers to manufacturers: Tesla is bundling car insurance into its vehicle sales in Australia and Hong Kong, and Volvo has said it would accept full liability for its self-driving cars.

Fewer people will own cars in the future, as well. Fleet-owned shared autonomous vehicles are expected to reduce the demand for personally owned cars and trucks by as much as 70 percent.

Regarding the disruption of auto insurance, however, we hold a view contrary to that of many analysts. We predict:

- **The driverless scenario will arrive on a less linear path** than the one typically projected. It will be decades before fully autonomous cars will fill the parking lots in any country—meaning that personal-line auto insurance will continue to exist.
- **The end of auto insurance is far off**, if it happens at all, but pressure will increase on cost structure. We agree with Accenture that premiums will decline in seven to ten years. Compensating for these losses to the industry will be new policies including cybersecurity insurance (covering theft, ransomware, remote hijacking, and losses caused by hacking such as identity theft and the misuse of personal information); product liability (covering manufacturers' liability for communication or Internet connection failure and for software and some hardware malfunctions), and infrastructure insurance (covering damages caused by the infrastructures controlling vehicle movements and traffic flow).

The Internet of Cars: telematics

Meanwhile, an increasing number of vehicles are already connected to the Internet. Some insurance carriers have entered the connected-car race. Technology does not drive these cars and trucks autonomously—yet—but aids drivers with GPS mapping and other features, while telematics reports to insurers where, when, and how they drive.

Telematics benefits the safe driver with lower premiums, and the insurer with information that enables better customer service and more accurate pricing via usage-based policies. It also creates a new paradigm, allowing any insurer to connect with clients and their risks.

And its popularity is growing. Octo Telematics announced in May 2017 that five million cars had connected to its platform worldwide, giving it almost 40 percent of the global telematics market, according to the IoT Insurance Observatory.

Telematics' benefits are a two-way street: Drivers like that it directly communicates to the insurer, including filling out claims forms with data collected from accidents, expediting claims processing. Insurers benefit from being able to use the data telematics generate to improve their bottom line and share this value with the customer. They also like being able to use the data to better serve customers and interact with them more frequently, and to increase their knowledge about their clients and their risks.

Some companies use telematics data to know when to provide push notifications that, for example, warn a driver when they are parking their vehicle in a less-safe area, and offer supplemental insurance until the car is moved. Being able to nudge the client to adopt less risky behaviors may also benefit the society as a whole.

Perhaps more important to those of us in the industry, the rapid and widespread adoption of telematics sends a warning to us: that we who do not offer it stand to lose relevance—and customers.

Here today, gone tomorrow: instant insurance

InsurTech is changing not just how insurance works, but when. A number of startups now offer "instant insurance" allowing customers to cover risks for limited periods.

We have created Neosurance, an early-stage startup focused on instant insurance delivered with a push approach (described in detail in Chapter 5 of this book). As of this writing, however, Trov, a California-based online provider founded in 2012, had attracted more investment capital than any other startup.

Trov offers on-demand property insurance that can cover a single item with the swipe of the user's smart phone, with premiums tailored accordingly. Its policies cover consumer electronics and photography equipment, but it planned to expand its offerings to insure jewelry, sporting goods, and other types of property that can be reliably priced.

Instant insurance challenges one of the traditional elements of mutuality: time. By insuring only the moments of exposure—the higher-risk moments—these policies remove the mutuality of who is exposed to the risk, and who is not.

Is insurance here to stay?

Real-time data, IoT, and AI pose challenges to many elements of the traditional insurance business model—but not in the way some may think.

In the future, when our "connected" refrigerator needs maintenance, will it purchase insurance to cover the cost of repairs? Will our smart watches prompt us to buy a policy before playing a sport? These so-called "smart" contracts may come to pass, but they aren't really insurance, not without risk transfer or randomness (accidental and unintentional loss).

We believe insurance is here to stay, and will continue to play a key role in the global economy. All these new technologies and sources of data will increase the quality of insurance risk classifications by creating smaller and more homogeneous classes. Clusterization will continue to prevail, as each class will still be characterized by an expected (but not certain) loss. And each individual will continue to bring expected risk to the portfolio.

At the portfolio level, therefore, mutuality will remain as the mechanism by which the premiums of many pay the claims of a few.

The end of the intermediary?

Artificial intelligence enables Trov, Lemonade, and other insurance startups to offer fast, easy coverage and claims without paperwork or human mediation. In a world that is getting increasingly digital and is becoming less about human interaction, the popularity of the chat bot over a human agent is understandable. But will artificial intelligence replace human intermediaries completely?

Online distribution may be the area most vulnerable to disruption in the insurance industry, Whitney Arthofer, a former associate at General Catalyst Partners, wrote in *TechCrunch* in 2016. Automating the complex underwriting process online, without paper documentation or in-person interaction, has not been a viable option in the past, she wrote, but things are changing fast thanks to new technologies and data sets.

Customer demand is driving this change, as in so many other sectors. The Internet, Arthofer wrote, provides "a new world of comparison shopping, online transactions and streamlined customer service." To succeed in this new world, she asserted, brokers need to hone their skills in three areas:

- **Direct marketing and consumer education:** best-in-class customer acquisition and engagement (content + advice) to build the brand and consumer trust;
- **Deep customer interactions:** the ability to facilitate the full transaction online; sophisticated CRM for personalization, retention and cross-sell; and expansion to mobile-native, and
- **Customer service:** (for lines that are more complex with large insured sets) deep product expertise, and dedicated support and claims management (mimicking the best of what offline agents offer).

Online insurance has existed for years, but has scaled up only in a few countries (such as the UK) and in a few insurance business lines (such as auto). Customers want what they want; not what we pretend they want. As a result, many insurance carriers are moving to an omni-channel customer experience with fully digital distribution.

But the day of the intermediary is not dead.

First of all, complex situations will continue to call for the expertise and guidance of trained and experienced people.

Second, non-compulsory insurance will still need to be sold.

As enthusiastic as we are about the possibilities for InsurTech, we feel skeptical about the ability of online distribution, comparison websites, and on-demand apps to adequately cover people's risk. To make wise decisions, customers need to be knowledgeable, rational, and focused, like Mr. Spock of "Star Trek" fame. In practice, however, many customers more closely resemble the cartoon character Homer Simpson—because they simply do not have enough information.

A growing number of InsurTech software and solutions may help agents better serve their customers, and improve efficiency and scalability—to stay relevant.

The future of insurance: one-stop shopping

Thus far, many startups are focusing their efforts on one or a few insurance lines. But the customer's expectations of finding everything they need in one place begs for all-inclusive insurance options, in which auto, home, hazard, health, property, cyber, pet, and other forms of insurance are bundled into one offering, with object- and time-specific "micro" insurance options available on demand. This approach may work especially well for businesses, which typically need several different types of insurance.

Compass Insurance serves as one example. The Colorado company offers home, auto, commercial, property, and other insurance products from more than fifteen companies. Far from being disintermediated, the company uses agents to help devise personalized, customized packages and comparison pricing. Keeping in mind the state's large population of outdoors enthusiasts, Compass even offers coverage of mountain bikes, snowboards, GPS devices and other outdoor gear—an innovative and decidedly customer-centric approach.

Of course, with these ideas comes opposition, with some citing regulatory and other obstacles to innovation. But the writing on the wall for the industry is clear: to remain relevant, we must be resilient.

We must find new ways to sell our products, and when necessary, create products to meet the needs of a market that is rapidly, and constantly, changing.

We must keep up with trends, ensuring that we have the same technologies that our customers have.

Rather than becoming entrenched in the way things have always been done, we must embrace the new and even be willing to take risks—a particular challenge in our risk-averse profession.

All signs point to continual shifting and morphing in the insurance arena, as in the world. Technology is a game-changer, and will someday be the default.

Darwinian evolution calls upon each of us in the industry to "adapt or die." In the insurance industry, "survival of the fittest" may well prove to mean "survival of the most resilient."

4

The three pillars of connected insurance

Motor, home, health

The world is getting bigger and smaller at the same time, and for the same reason: technology. Computers have become a ubiquitous part of everyday life, expanding our world to include people and businesses around the world even while they connect us ever more intimately with those nearby and even with ourselves, as well as with our homes, workplaces, possessions, banks, retailers, and increasingly, insurers—making up, altogether, our connected "ecosystem."

Today, there is more than one connected device per person in the world, and by some estimates the figure will reach seven devices per person by 2020. (Cisco Internet Business Solutions Group estimates seven per person; AIG/CEA estimates five per person.) Others put the number at fifty devices for a family of four by 2022. The insurance sector cannot stop this trend; we can only figure out how to deal with it.

While technology makes it imperative that we keep pace with the changes affecting our customers' lives, it also provides us unparalleled opportunities to innovate and add value to what we are offering. One thing is clear: falling behind is not an option. We ignore the digital revolution at our own peril. To thrive in this profession in the coming years, every insurance player must be InsurTech.

Adapt or perish

Being connected has become the talk of the town, and insurance companies are surely one of the main interested parties in this discussion—especially those who promote change and innovation. "Traditional" players who cling to the status quo will have a tougher time adapting to this paradigm shift. To remain competitive, they must adjust to the new rules of the game.

The name of that game is "connected insurance": insurance solutions using sensors to collect data on the state of an insured risk, and telematics for remote transmission and management of that data.

Consumers are becoming more and more connected at home, at work, behind the wheel, engaging in sports and leisure activities, and so on. The "internet of things" is coming quickly, and companies must be able to react accordingly to maximize value for their clients and for themselves.

Not only are our phones getting smarter; so is our surrounding environment—our "things." This connected ecosystem creates new avenues of potential growth for insurance companies, most notably in how we analyze and use the data these devices generate. How can we read the numbers to identify patterns, and use data to control losses, perfect risk assessment and prevention, and better serve our customers?

Telematics: a case study

No matter what our insurance line, we can learn a lot from automotive insurance's use of telematics, a technology already front-and-center in the InsurTech field. "Telematics"—the word blends "telecommunication" and "informatics"—is a system in which devices capture, store, analyze, and transmit data produced by sensors and connected things. Working primarily via a "black box" installed in a vehicle, telematics is one of the first connected insurance technologies.

Telematics holds promise for non-automotive uses, as well. For a bird's-eye view of insurance in the age of connectedness, we must also consider the ramifications for home and health as well as motor insurance, and try to address limits and opportunities, business P&L, and, of course, customers, who are, after all, the most important piece of the "connected" puzzle.

Contrary to popular belief, the insurance industry is not completely averse to change.

Remote insurance sales date as far back as the early 1980s, when the German Post Office first experimented using Bildschirmtext, which transmitted data through telephone lines and displayed the content on a television screen.

In the UK today, nearly sixty percent of auto insurance coverage is sold online, and comparison websites are the "normal" way to purchase an auto insurance policy.

Motor insurance telematics leads the industry in innovation around the world. A South African player, Discovery, is one of the first to show that the technology, if managed correctly, can change behaviors, benefitting the insurer's P&L, the customer, and society. Discovery's "Vitalitydrive" rewards drivers with discounts on fuel purchases for driving knowledge, driving course attendance, and driving practices.

In the race to the telematics top, Italy leads the way, in part because of its strong automotive industry. The nation's insurers were early adopters of telematics, pioneering the technology beginning in 2002. Although it was expensive, high insurance rates helped the market absorb the costs.

Other countries are beginning to see telematics insurance policies, as well, including the U.S., UK, South Africa, Austria, Canada and, most recently, Germany. In the near future, newcomers including Brazil, China, and Russia are expected to play "catch-up," and are now accelerating toward the exploration phase.

North America has been a slow adopter. In 2016, around 3.5 million cars in the United States sent data to an insurance company in some way, representing less than 1.5 percent of the market. In Canada, about 500,000 vehicles use telematics. While the number of users in both countries is growing, it falls far behind Italy's penetration rate.

Nearly 20 percent of Italian auto insurance policies sold and renewed in the last quarter of 2016 had a telematics device provided by an insurer, according to the Italian Institute for the Supervision of Insurance (IVASS). The IoT Insurance Observatory estimated that, by September of 2017, 7 million Italian customers had a telematics policy.

Some insurers are using telematics data to create value, and share this value with customers. The most successful products with the largest traction include three elements:

- An insurer-provided device that the customer installs on the battery, under the car's hood;
- A 20 percent up-front, flat discount on annual auto liability premiums, and
- A suite of additional services—stolen vehicle recovery, car finder, weather alerts—for a fee of about €50, charged to the customer.

Although use-based insurance (UBI) is most often cited in connection with telematics, the above approach does not qualify as UBI. Instead, it works only to satisfy the customer's most relevant needs, including:

- **Saving money** on a compulsory product. Research shows that consumers consider price when choosing insurance.
- **Receiving support** and convenience at the moment of truth—the claims moment. Insurers are providing a better post-crash customer experience using telematics data, gathering information without having to question the client.
- **Receiving services** other than insurance. That's something roughly 60 percent of insurance customers look forward to and value, according to recent research from Bain.

Let's analyze this approach from an economic perspective:

- **The fee to the customer is nearly the same as the cost for the hardware and services.** The €50 fee mentioned above represents more than 5 percent of the insurance premium for risky clients paying an annual premium higher than €1,000—who make up less than 5 percent of the Italian telematics market. The fee is more than ten percent of the premium for customers

paying less than €400—more than 40 percent of the Italian telematics market.
- **The product is a constant, daily presence in the car, with no possibility of turning it off.** While it ensures support in case of a crash, it also deters fraudulent claims and risky driving behaviors.
- **The telematics portfolio has shown, on average, 20 percent fewer claims** than the non-telematics portfolio on a risk-adjusted basis, according to the Italian Association of Insurers.
- **Insurer best practices have achieved additional savings on claims costs** with a proactive claims management approach. The process begins as soon as a crash happens, and uses an objective reconstruction of the crash dynamic to support the claim handler's decisions.
- **The customer receives a suite of telematics services along with a 25 percent up-front discount** on the auto liability premium.

Value, value, value

Carriers concerned about the price of telematics technology can maximize their ROI using the practices outlined above. Savvy insurers use black-box data to add value in three areas: services purchased by the customer, risk selection, and loss control. By offering an up-front discount, they share this added value with the customer. In Italy, the most successful players achieved a telematics penetration of almost 40 percent, and their telematics portfolios continue to grow.

These insurers have orchestrated an ecosystem of partners to deliver a "customer-centric" auto insurance value proposition. In contrast to approaches being tried in insurance lines around the world—where the value proposition is simply enlarged by adding some services—this InsurTech approach also uses the insurers' unique competitive advantage—the insurance technical P&L—to create a virtuous, value-sharing mechanism based on telematics data.

The story of the Italian auto telematics market shows how InsurTech adoption can strengthen the insurance sector and help it protect the ways in which people live and organizations work. Although used primarily in motor vehicles today, telematics could prove one of the most relevant digital innovations in the entire insurance industry, used throughout the "Internet of Everything" to transmit data to insurers in several different lines, including **home** and **health**—the other two "pillars" coming of age in the connected insurance industry.

There's no place like home

We stand at the beginning of a journey that will be shaped by technology, interconnectivity, and privacy and security implications, particularly as they apply to the Internet of Things (IoT). The use of telematics is expanding beyond automobiles to cover our homes.

Growth in the home insurance market will continue with the number of connected home devices including security cameras, televisions, thermostats, appliances, and virtual personal assistants such as Amazon's Alexa and Apple's Siri. Every transaction using these devices generates information that could be useful to insurance providers for:

- **Preventing and mitigating risks.** Smart-home sensors might detect plumbing leaks, alerting insurer and insured alike before costly damage occurs. They could call firefighters to the scene of a fire before the homeowner even smells smoke. They might alert the insurer to the home dweller's plans to go on vacation, allowing the insurer to send a reminder to buy traveler's insurance.
- **Improving the underwriting claims process.** Using data generated by home devices offers enormous potential for increased effectiveness and efficiency of underwriting and claims processing, especially where premiums are higher than $800.

- **Increasing relevance to the customer.** IoT could enable insurers to offer tailored, specific policies at the most relevant and meaningful times.

The connected world promises to reshape and redefine the risk landscape, not only in homes but also in commercial enterprises. In both environments, sensors can combine to produce, in effect, a real-time warning dashboard. A homeowner or enterprise risk manager can have at their fingertips an interactive risk management system with alerts from things "communicating" their use, status, and damage—and sending claim notices automatically to insurers, who then may create initial claim reserves and assign the right claim adjusters, all automatically.

From "connected" home to "smart" home

The technology website CNET describes a "smart" home as "a home that is equipped with network-connected products (i.e., 'smart products,' connected via wi-fi, Bluetooth or similar protocols) for controlling, automating and optimizing functions such as temperature, lighting, security, safety or entertainment, either remotely by a phone, tablet, or computer, or a separate system within the home itself.

"The home must have a smart security feature or a smart temperature feature in addition to a reliable internet connection. It then must include at least two features from a list of smart options, including appliances, entertainment, lighting, outdoor sensors, and safety detectors."

The first step toward a "smart" home is a "connected" home. Your home can be "connected" if it has wiring or wireless infrastructure that enables devices to communicate with each other and with the Internet or cloud.

For reaching "smart home" status, you need a system that coordinates all connected devices to work as a single unit. A smart home that is truly useful would also tend to other needs such as health and wellness and baby monitoring, besides security and consumption monitoring.

The smart-home trend, although slow to catch on at first, is spreading quickly now. Some 8.4 billion connected things were expected to be in use worldwide in 2017, rising to 20.4 billion by 2020, according to a report from Gartner. Greater China, North America and western Europe were expected to comprise two-thirds of the market.

One likely reason for the growth: falling prices. The cost of sensors has dropped to an average of 60 cents each, a decline of more than 50 percent over the past decade, according to CBInsights.

Interestingly, U.S. smart home adoption is lagging behind that of international markets. Deal shares to international smart-home startups have seen a significant rise in recent years.

Security: a barrier to adoption

The main issues standing in the way of the smart home are security and privacy, costs, and confusion over how to integrate the various products into a single household system.

Often, a consumer will buy several devices for the home thinking they will work together, only to find that they do not. The mistake can be a costly one: surveys done by Italy's Osservatori.net show that expense was the main reason people did not own home-connected devices.

Even among those in the know, however, security and privacy remain formidable obstacles to establishing a smart home. With so many devices lacking even basic security features, the risks are many, and very real.

An interconnected world is one where our home appliance and security systems exchange information with our mobile devices, computer, wearables, appliances, and car. All these connections mean added access points for cybercriminals.

Already, automobiles have proven to be hackable, and controllable, by an outside agent. A home may be a less-hazardous environment, but the threat is still real. Entry to one sensor or device can provide access to all.

During the Insurance IoT USA Summit Chicago in December 2016, Dean Weber, CTO at Mocana, made a great case for why the public, regulators and device manufacturers should analyze the issue with utmost care. For example, an October 2015 hack of connected security cameras and DVRs resulted in a widespread shutdown of some major websites including Twitter, Netflix, Spotify and Airbnb. What stands in the way of anyone's hacking into our home?

Creating truly secure technology for the IoT is crucial. At the same time, however, the connected world's weakness may prove to be the insurance industry's strength. Risk, after all, is what we know best, and are best equipped to protect the consumer from. How might we fill this gap to not only cover breaches and their costs but also help our customers mitigate risk?

The third pillar: healthcare

Cyberattacks also pose a major concern in healthcare. Connected medical devices as well as systems containing personal information stand to be breached by cybercriminals, potentially wreaking personal and financial havoc, if not death. Again, we in the insurance field must be ready with policies to protect patients and healthcare providers, and with managed-risk programs to help prevent intrusions in the first place.

At the same time, insurers must stay abreast of changing and shifting trends in healthcare, which is undergoing a transformation at this very moment. Health insurers are trying to transition from their traditional "payer" role to a more central one in which customers turn to them for help with health-related matters, in other words a "player".

Wearables, 'm-health,' and telemedicine are just a few technologies on the leading edge of the connected healthcare trend, one sure to grow because connectivity benefits everyone: insurers and insured.

Consider, for example, the high costs of treating patients with chronic ailments and of caring for the elderly. Insurers may control losses by focusing on less-risky clients, offering them a customized value proposition that they can't refuse. To do so, they will need to create a network of partners that allows them to diversify and manage profitability levels. By concentrating on young customers, who are healthier and device-smart, companies can use such strategies as gamification to generate loyalty, guide behavior, and focus on prevention instead of reaction—thus controlling losses.

Connected healthcare also will be influenced by emerging models such as "seamless" care (using technology to smoothly transition patients from hospital to home), "shared" care (in which all members of a group contribute to provide care for one another), "collaborative" care (in which medical professionals of differing disciplines work together) and home hospitals. These customer-centric models demonstrate the industry's move away from the patriarchal "doctor-patient" model to one that empowers the consumer.

Connected health stands to play a major role in shaping the future of healthcare and of health insurance. Connected insurance involves more than connecting insurers with data; it also connects insurers with people and their risk. To compete in this new game, insurers must create new customer experiences.

From 'patient' to 'consumer'

To create solid relationships with our customers, we must consider them first. We must listen to and understand them, including their emotions and needs, and engage frequently using many touch points, including digital ones. Then we must design customer journeys based on ecosystems of services, and use new available technologies to meet those needs.

Many insurers already create partnerships to become more specialized. Most are not so great, however, at analyzing the data all these connections produce, or at creating efficient customer experiences. Legacy systems are certainly not helpful when designing innovative solutions for the market.

Innovators in health insurance should aim to transform the insurance company from a payer to a proactive player in the customer health journey.

The industry has to take a step backward in the customer journey, passing from a "cure" to a "care" approach. We can differentiate insurance coverage by client segments, and offer services such as medical information, a call center for emergencies, and online ordering and home delivery of pharmaceutical products.

We can also provide e-health services such as monitoring and alert devices for elderly patients and those with chronic conditions such as heart problems or diabetes.

Thanks to connected healthcare, practitioners can advise their patients in a number of ways including messaging, calls, and video. Insurers can propose discounted prices through a preferred network, while providing the option of booking and paying online. And why not offer patients their complete medical history in a digital format for easy use by doctors and clinics?

Keeping with insurers' new role as risk preventers, we might try gamification using data from wearables with tailor-made goals; wellness content in multiple formats; and agreements with gyms, shops and other types of service providers.

Technology offers great potential for the health insurer, including the ability to solicit and serve less-risky clients and present them with an improved, better-priced product. But insurers will need to partner with technology innovators and medical providers, keeping in mind that our role in the health system is changing from "payer" to "player."

Connected insurance in the health sector affects the entire insurance value chain and generates real value for insurance P&L. The five main value creation levers are:

- **Behavior "steering" programs,** leading the client toward less-risky behaviors to improve their health and reduce claims;
- **Value-added services**, developing client-tailored ancillary services that allow the insurer to serve as an omni-channel medical "concierge";
- **Loss control,** developing a broad approach to claims mitigation including:
    - an "early warning" system capable of anticipating serious health problems and more expensive claims;
    - e-health and m-health technologies able to reduce health-care costs, and
    - improved reimbursement valuation, thanks to a more efficient and faster claims management process that allows the insurer to be more present, and increases the speed and efficiency of claims, limiting the portfolio loss ratio;
- **Risk selection,** creating a value proposition that attracts less risky clients or enhances the underwriting phase with temporary monitoring by dedicated devices; and
- **Dynamic risk-based pricing,** developing insurance policies with pricing linked to individual risks and behaviors. This model reduces premium leaks while offering lower prices to low-risk individuals, increasing customer acquisitions and retention.

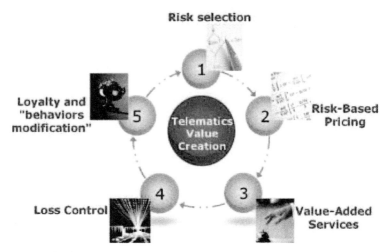

Image 2. *The five main value creation levers*

Data collection can improve the underwriting process by allowing price adjustments or covenants, and also create pricing linked to risk. Devices can measure client behaviors and collect data to customize coverage and propose individual prices or discounts, generating an impressive refinement of the traditional risk-classification model —one that will grow increasingly sustainable as technology continues to evolve.

The opportunity to change customer behaviors is the "elephant in the room." Behavior programs use information about client behaviors to direct them toward less-risky solutions, using reward systems and gamification programs to motivate safer, healthier choices.

The Vitality program created by the South African insurance company Discovery provides one of the best examples of how to build a highly competitive business model by appealing to younger, healthier clients.

First, the program evaluates the customer's health using traditional methods and wearables, and creates a personal improvement plan. As an incentive to follow the plan, it offers discounts for use of "health partners" including gyms, healthy food providers, and sellers of wearables and other devices, and rewards points to customers for "healthy" behaviors. To encourage loyalty, the company also pays back 20 percent of the annual premium to long-time clients.

Technology = value

Connected auto, home, and health insurance form the foundation for a new way of doing business industry-wide. Next up, we expect: workers' compensation and industrial risk.

Value sharing is the heart of connected insurance: the motor that drives the engine. Whatever the business line, insurers can apply the five "value creation levers" outlined above, using the data from connected devices to not only generate value on insurance P&L but also to share this value through incentives, services and discounts. The result will be not only added value for insurers and customers, but also for society as a whole as individual behaviors change, reducing overall risk.

Connected insurance is a new paradigm that can take the insurance sector to the next level. The business model and even the role of insurance companies are not so much changed by technology's evolution as enlarged by it.

Since the creation of the first insurance policy more than seven hundred years ago, insurance's essential functions have consisted of assessing, managing and transferring risks. Now, thanks to the "superpower" that is technology, we can do it all so much better—if we not only accept InsurTech and embrace it, but *become* it.

5

Micro insurance: engaging customers

In the right way, at the right time

In developing countries, people often cannot afford or may not need blanket insurance policies for homes, cars, health, and life. For them, micro insurance is touted as the "next big thing."

This innovative insurance, which provides very specific coverage for limited periods at a low cost, holds great promise for more affluent nations, as well. Increasingly popular with younger age groups, its customer-centric approach—letting the insured choose the what, when, and how much—not only works well for a variety of lifestyles, but also may provide unique opportunities for insurers to close gaps in protection and even to create new products. And InsurTech has a major role to play.

But micro insurance does seem especially well-suited for "third-world" or lower-income nations, where the potential market is estimated at 1.5 to three billion new policies. In Africa and Asia as well as some economies in South and Central America, "developing" economies comprise 70 percent of the world's seven billion people.

In these nations, the demand is high for certain types of insurance including health, life, agricultural, property, and catastrophic coverage. About 135 million people have micro insurance, just 5 percent of the potential market—leaving plenty of room for more, even with an average annual growth rate of 10 percent.

Micro finance and micro credit are also popular offerings in developing countries. But micro insurance's business potential differs in important ways.

Micro finance offers low-income households access to high-quality financial services, including credit, savings, insurance, and fund transfers. Micro credit, thought to have originated with Bangladesh's Grameen Bank in 1983, provides credit services to those with low incomes, making very small loans to impoverished borrowers who typically lack collateral, steady employment, and a verifiable credit history.

Why cater to poor people? Because, when offered the right products, means and knowledge, they can become effective consumers of financial services. The Micro insurance Centre estimates that in the next ten years or so, the micro insurance market could grow to one billion policyholders, representing a third of the potential market.

The possibilities are enormous, but only if we do not take for granted the demand for our products and services. Insurance can have a poor reputation in the developing world. To win customers, the industry needs an innovative approach that includes customer education and incentives.

Teaching the basics

When resources are already stretched thin, people may wonder whether insurance is worth the cost. They may not understand why they even need it. We can inform them and develop their trust using popular media—perhaps TV and radio programs portraying insurance's helping a family rebuild after a flood, for example, or a farmer's wishing they had bought insurance when drought decimates the crop. Insurance-sponsored literacy campaigns also can help boost the industry's image, and people's trust.

To create demand for insurance, we might encourage government incentives such as tax exemptions, subsidies, and compulsory coverage. But for micro insurance to work well in a developing economy, we must keep the products and processes simple, and the premiums low. We may need to change our mindset as well as our administration strategies and distribution channels.

And we may need to ask ourselves new questions: How do we sell insurance to someone who has never bought it before? How do we generate revenues from a policy whose premium is just a few dollars per year?

New solutions for developing countries are starting to emerge, such as in parts of Asia, where pre-pay cards provide insurance coverage for flood damage. Insurers will need to find the right business model and partners when approaching these markets, and must consider new mechanisms for controlling moral hazard, adverse selection, and fraud. Proxy underwriting, group policies, and waiting periods may mitigate adverse selection, for instance.

Investing in micro insurance might seem risky, but doing so will reap returns: reputational gain in the short term; knowledge in the medium term, and, in the long term, growth.

If micro insurance is to enter developing economies, we must give more thought to critical areas: product innovation and technological solutions that are adapted to low income markets; choosing the right partners to work with such as NGOs, community-based organizations, and international reinsurers, and understanding the risk factors that will affect the region in the future: economic development, climate change, and population growth trends, to name a few.

Going mobile: opportunities abound

People in developing countries are most likely to use mobile technologies, especially phones. This is true in developed nations, as well: more than half the world's population uses a mobile phone today, and nearly one-quarter uses the Internet regularly. In the developing world, the number of people who say they own a smart phone and use the Internet has increased significantly in recent years, according to the Pew Research Center. And fewer than 5 percent of low-income people have access to insurance or to coverage that they actually need.

Moreover, in nearly every country, millennials—those who are now between 18 and 34—are much more likely to use the Internet and smart phones than are people over 35. They are also the most underinsured generation: the least likely to have health, rental, life, or disability insurance.

This gap, plus the rapid adoption of mobile technologies around the world, represents a huge opportunity for the insurance industry, especially for new kinds of micro insurance.

Since its introduction in 2010 by the widely known Asian insurer Tokio Marine, micro insurance has been ripe for innovation. Some players have developed stand-alone, on-demand solutions with mobile apps. Others have partnered with other players to set up a B2B2C approach, using incidental channels to reach customers.

The insurance connection

As we have seen, connected insurance is mainly about people: how to reach and engage with them efficiently and effectively, and at the same time help them connect their risks with the coverage they choose. Connected insurance, with its access to a broad range of data, provides never-before-seen insights into our customers' behaviors and lifestyles. And, as we have noted, benefits to the insurance sector include increased knowledge about clients and their risks.

In this innovative landscape, micro insurance offers a transversal opportunity for insurers to use that knowledge, move closer to their clients, and offer the right coverage at the right time.

"Insurance is sold, not bought," as we have noted, is a popular saying in our industry, and it is still true. And non-compulsory coverage is the only thing more difficult to sell! New technologies, however, offer new ways to incentivize purchases, including using innovative push notifications to alert customers to policy needs they did not even know they had.

At the same time, we want to avoid annoying customers with offers that do not interest them—the wrong insurance, at the wrong time. Using data collection and analytics to gain insight into their lifestyles and preferences can help ensure that our offers are timely and relevant.

For an example, let's look at Neosurance, an InsurTech startup that we, its founder and an investor, are well-positioned to boast about. Neosurance is unique in the field of "one-time insurance." Its technology platform is an advanced artificial intelligence agent that matches context, insurance needs, and the right insurance coverage—in milliseconds.

Neosurance's "Virtual Insurance Agent" is designed to formulate its "sales pitch" according to the context and the personal attitude of each customer, just as a skilled human agent would do. This technology, integrated into existing mobile apps, sends insurance suggestions to more than 800,000 customers in Europe and the U.S.

A 50/50 joint venture between Neosperience, specialists in Digital Customer Experience, and Digital Tech International, operating in the InsurTech sector, Neosurance aims to create a new insurance market.

Often, customers are not only underinsured, they are also unaware that they may need coverage, or that the opportunities for it exist. Like a knowledgeable, capable insurance agent, Neosurance stimulates the need for protection with push notifications on the customer's smart phone, stimulating impulse purchases of small-ticket insurance.

The 'push' for attention

With the average person's attention span dropping from twelve seconds in 2000 to eight seconds in 2013, many of us now have shorter spans than goldfish do—a change attributed at least in part to mobile technology. Rather than bemoan the difficulties of engaging our customers, however, perhaps we ought to explore the opportunities these technologies offer, and how to use them to grab the customer's attention.

We think insurance should adapt to the customer's habits and environment. The best way to do that is by using this "push" approach to sell micro insurance that will cover a specific instantaneous need. Know what the customer needs before they do! Then, you'll be positioned to provide the right insurance coverage at precisely the right moment.

A good micro insurance solution should create a seamless digital customer experience. It does that by reading and interpreting customer behaviors and emotions. The aim here is to create a "win-win" situation for customers and insurers alike—which push micro insurance does, beautifully.

The smart phone is no longer just a channel; it has become a proxy of the customer. Just as agents know their clients, Neosurance's artificial intelligence engine learns and gathers in-depth knowledge about customers by tracking behaviors, context, and even emotions—all channeled through the smart phone. So, rather than just pushing messages to customer segments (i.e. "women 25 to 35"), Neosurance's technology can create a continuous cycle of insight-driven, highly personalized contextual interactions.

For the consumer, push micro insurance keeps the insurer close at hand when the customer needs protection, offering the convenience of buying personalized micro insurance on the spot, directly from the smart phone.

Neosurance delivers the right insurance at the right time for a beautifully simple mobile experience that meets customer needs. It lifts the insurance sales process to the next level, potentially transforming every insurance company into an InsurTech. In essence, Neosurance's disruption stems not only from technology, but from a new mindset.

Customer-centric: the new mindset

That mindset is customer focus. Neosurance uses technology to overcome barriers and deliver products and services faster and at a lower cost than incumbents can do. It is innovative and fast, relying on digital ecosystems to find the data, technology, distribution platforms, and skills needed to fill the gaps in their own capabilities. It combines traditional revenue streams with digital business models, which treat all business capabilities—data, technology platforms, and access to customers—as assets that can be monetized.

So, what's the magic combination for winning the attention of customers, especially those underinsured millenials? The key to selling insurance to millennials is to reach them with the right message, at the right time, on a device they swipe, tap and pinch 2,617 times a day.

And millennials are just the tip of the iceberg. The "connected generation," which includes Generation Y, is the single most important customer segment. Empowered by technology, these users search out services that they can use across platforms and screens.

It's time for a new distribution paradigm for the insurance sector. When coverage is not compulsory, we must stimulate the emotional need for protection. Using artificial intelligence to deliver a push suggestion at the right time with the right offer, providing a simple process for making a purchase, and offering an easy-to-understand contract: this is the wave of the future. Insurers, reinsurers, and startups, working together, must create new insurance propositions while developing a streamlined purchasing process.

Win-win-win partnerships

Neosurance's job is to identify communities (homogenous groups of people already aggregated by a community owner) and to partner with insurers who are able and willing to provide insurance coverage that fits with each community experience. Integrating Neosurance's platform enables insurers to deliver sales proposals that become more and more accurate, based on the single user's context and behavior.

Why does this matter? Consumers often have difficulty understanding what insurers are offering because insurance contracts are complex and difficult to follow. People wonder if what they are buying suits them individually, or even meets their needs. Other industries have done a much better job of making their customers feel cared for and catered to, and of using technology to heighten those perceptions. How can we learn from them?

Mass insurance is becoming obsolete. As technology makes it possible to customize, today's consumer demands it in all areas of life and business. Newcomers to the insurance industry are using tech to shift the model toward context and utility. These newcomers are shaking things up, offering fresh and even disruptive alternatives to the incumbent's way of doing business. A deep collaboration between incumbents and InsurTech startups to deliver innovative solutions is one of the most oft-predicted trends, and we're already starting to see some great examples.

InsurTechs have great potential in the insurance field, even if traditional insurers still make the rules—at this point, after all, insurers own the capital, infrastructure, and industry knowledge. But if traditionals want to keep the upper hand, they must embrace InsurTech startups' solutions. These startups are legacy-system-free, resourceful, and creative, but they usually lack in-depth knowledge about the insurance sector. If more insurers were to join in partnership with them, everyone would stand to gain—insurers, tech startups, and consumers.

How do insurers benefit from teaming up with the new kids on the block? By learning about new technologies and incorporating them into their business models, they remain relevant in our increasingly tech-centered world. They must become InsurTechs, or fade away. How better to achieve this pivot than by working closely with the newcomers?

Micro insurance: an investor's dream

As previously noted, micro insurance can reduce the protection gap in developing countries as well as appeal to millennials, who often would rather interact with their phones than with traditional intermediaries.

But micro insurance also holds the power to revolutionize insurance sales.

Here's why: micro insurance not only delivers innovation to customers, but it helps insurers gain insights into their clients so they can address their needs without second-guessing.

Its applications could be huge. And the data it collects and analyzes brings added value to both insurer and customer. Altogether, this niche poses an almost irresistible allure to investors.

As with all financial-services business lines, insurance providers can now use sophisticated data and insights to provide highly personalized products that meet consumers' increasingly specific expectations. The sharing economy demands niche products, and only those relevant to customers' use and behavior patterns will remain successful.

As we have seen, Italy offers the worldwide leading-edge experience in car insurance innovation, and is the only market where auto insurance telematics is already mainstream. This incredible performance has been possible thanks to collaboration between insurers and tech companies. InsurTech allows the insurance industry to collect data using black boxes, analyze that data, and use it to select risks and improve claims management.

This virtuous collaboration between incumbents and tech players inspired us to found Neosurance. Positioned as an enabler for traditional carriers to take advantage of the huge opportunities presented by micro insurance, our startup has gained international traction.

For the insurer, instant insurance is still uncharted territory, with much to be explored. Many on-demand apps on the market appear to risk "adverse selection," turning off consumers rather than inspiring them to turn on coverage—and even approaching them after an event has already occurred. In contrast, Neosurance's push approach appears to be effective and sustainable.

Avoiding adverse selection is key to protecting profitability, and using the digital sales force to sell policies in a smart way via artificial intelligence and machine learning. Push micro insurance allows us to reach the "connected generation" right where they like to spend most of their time—on their smart phones–while minimizing the risk of antiselection.

Neosurance's instant-push insurance approach offers a great example of how technologists and insurers can work together in a customer-centric partnership. Technologies such as these are moving the insurance sales process to the next level, potentially transforming every old insurance company into an InsurTech.

6
Our InsurTech predictions

Everyone enjoys predicting trends, and now is an especially exciting time to look ahead in our field. Technology is rapidly changing the world, and to many in the often-staid insurance industry, it's time *we* changed, as well. But how will the transformation occur, and what shape will it take? Or—will it truly change at all?

Specialized portals, social networks, and artificial agents will help create awareness of insurance needs, some say. Others point to front-end changes that have already occurred such as apps, chatbots, and instant underwriting, and say we should expect more of the same. Skeptics, however, assert that these additions to the value chain are largely superficial, leaving policies and coverage types basically untouched. Where is the transformation our industry so badly needs?

The future of the insurance industry is certainly uncertain—but technology's advance into the field has only recently begun. Not long ago, analysts bemoaned a lack of InsurTech startups. Over the last two years, however, venture capitalists have pumped almost $7 million into InsurTech, and some 380 InsurTech startups have emerged in the last four years, according to an FT Partners analysis.

And although it seemed unlikely for a while, predictions that distribution would drive industry transformations may now be coming true. InsurTech startups are finding new ways to bring insurance to consumers, McKinsey & Company reports: 37 percent of them are focusing their efforts on distribution.

A changing industry

Digital transformation is leaving its mark in four macro areas:
- **Consumer expectations.** More than 75 percent of consumers say they expect to use a digital channel for insurance interactions in addition to traditional approaches, according to a recent survey by Bain & Company. Not having your own app or mobile-friendly website offering

digital transactions is no longer an option for any insurance company that hopes to survive. Omni-channel customer journeys are here to stay.
- **Product flexibility.** The traditional Japanese player Tokio Marine offers temporary insurance policies via mobile phone: travel insurance that provides coverage only on the dates when the client is traveling, for instance, and personal accident coverage for people playing a sport only while they are in the game. The Italian company Neosurance, too, offers micro insurance, a growing field that holds great promise. Customers like the flexibility and lower cost this solution provides, and will certainly flock to this form of insurance as time goes on.
- **Ecosystems**. Exciting things can happen when an insurance value proposition collaborates with partners from other sectors.
- **Services.** The old, risk-based plan is under disruption. Insurers are moving, instead, toward more comprehensive plans that include additional services, such as weather alerts and emergency responder notifications in case of a crash. People will continue to want more bang for their insurance buck, as technology allows them to do in all aspects of life today.

In the rearview mirror

For fun, let's look at how Matteo's Christmas 2016 predictions fared in the first three quarters of 2017:
- **Exit.** *Prediction*: Not everyone will prosper. Although many amazing InsurTech companies are seeing great results and scaling up—and many will continue to enter the field—some will surely leave the game, as well.
Result: Matteo was dreaming of an InsurTech unicorn's exit. Well, dreams become reality sometimes: Well Zong An – the Chinese full stack InsurTech – made its IPO with a $10 billion evaluation in fall

2017. Also, Travelers acquired Symply Business for $400M. On the other hand, Guevara left the game in the second half of the year. This winnowing down, a Darwinian "survival of the fittest," should ultimately strengthen our industry.

- **Reconversion**: This is the other side of the "exit" moon. *Prediction*: We have witnessed many initiatives putting together a fantastic team, a sexy equity story and terrific fundraising, but using business models that appear, to us, unsustainable from an insurance perspective—they don't pass the "Four Ps" test we outlined in Chapter 2. We don't want to claim that none will succeed: far be it from us to engage in skepticism during such an unpredictable era. Instead, we expect to see some of these players use their great skills and the funds they have raised to radically change their business models.

  Result: In spring 2017, Trov did a round of financing of more of $40 million with an evaluation higher than $300 million, but from what we heard from the CEO at different conferences, the company is focusing its efforts on a back-end system that insurers can use on their customer base rather than on growing its customer base and portfolio of on-demand risks. Also, Zenefit went through a difficult 2017, stepped back from the brokerage business, and started to license its technology as an SaaS (Software as a Service) player.

- **Connected insurance**: *Prediction*: Our money is on any insurance solution that uses sensors to collect data on the state of an insured risk, and telematics to remotely transmit and manage that data on the insurance value chain. A crazy prediction? Let's consider the most mature use case: auto insurance telematics in Italy, representing one of the best practices globally, in which 4.8 million cars were digitally connected to an insurance provider at the end of 2015. Matteo predicted that the number of vehicles "connected" with an insurer in Italy would top 7.5 million by the end of 2017.

Result: In line with the expectations, Italy's insurance telematics policies had reached 7 million by the end of third quarter 2017, according to the IoT Insurance Observatory.

- **Culture shift**: *Prediction*: Not all legacy insurers will resist change. Incumbents appear increasingly interested in debating innovations and testing new approaches, including collaborating with startups. Matteo expected to see this new breeze surround old-style insurance institutions as more of them realized the importance of InsurTech to their own future, and to that of the industry.

    Result: A board member at one of the largest global reinsurers recently summarized the essence of insurance as assessing, dealing, and accepting risks using the latest technologies. That's one sign that the industry is coming around. We saw 3,800 more signs at InsurTech Connect, the world's most prestigious InsurTech conference. In 2016, the conference had 1,200 participants; in October 2017, it sold out with more than 3,800 attendees. We were there on the stage, and witnessed the incredible energy of those insurance professionals, regulators and startups.

- **Sustainability**: *Prediction*: Many value propositions will bundle risk coverage and services. Doing so allows the insurer to influence behaviors and prevent risk, thereby contributing to the sustainability of the insurance sector and sharing value with the society in general. Matteo expected to see some insurers becoming more relevant in the lives of their clients, acting not only as claim payers, but also as "players"—partners in their customers' life and behavioral choices, generating benefits to society.

    Result: The speeches of top insurance executives speeches show the sector's ambition to go in this direction. A slide projected on a wall is just that, however: in the field, we see very few examples of implementation.

Nothing happens overnight in the insurance sector, as we have noted many times in this book. But our slow pace may also give us an advantage, allowing us to reconnoiter from time to time, adjust our vision, and peer farther—and, perhaps, more accurately—into the future. What will happen in coming years? Matteo is working with his crystal ball.

The greatest challenge

How can insurers assimilate InsurTech start-ups and technologies into their value chains? This will be the greatest challenge.

We must figure out how to integrate user experiences and data sources. Frankly, it would be untenable to have dozens of specialized partners with different apps cluttering the insurer's main policy offerings. We will need, instead, to manage this expansion and fragmentation of the new insurance value chain.

To solve this problem, some firms are creating new ways to collaborate. It is a daunting task, this integration and management of data, devices, apps, sensors, and expectations to provide not only superior customer service and great insurance coverage, but also new and dynamic ways for our own industry to do more, be more, and matter more. One thing we know is this: we cannot stop progress. Technology affects us all, and will do so increasingly. Keeping up—or, even better, getting ahead of the curve—must be our goal, now and in the future.

And this brings us full circle to the very first sentence of this book. Predicting the future is tricky, but we do not need Matteo's crystal ball to know what lies ahead for our industry. In the future—sooner than we might think—all insurance players will be InsurTech, meaning players will use technology as key enabler to achieve their strategic goals. Those that are not InsurTech will go home. When that day comes, where will you be?

References

1. Bateman, Milford. *Why Doesn't Microfinance Work? The Destructive Rise of Local Neoliberalism.* Zed Books, 2010.
2. Carbone, Matteo. "Connecting the dots through insurance", November 2017, http://ezine.business-reporter.co.uk/november-2017-future-of-insurance#!/opening-shots.
3. Carbone, Matteo. "Will Fintech Disrupt Health, Home Firms?" Insurance Thought Leadership, 7 August 2015 (http:// insurancethoughtleadership.com/will-fintech-disrupt-health-home-insurers).
4. Carbone, Matteo. "Insurtech is the way to keep the insurance sector relevant", 20 July 2017, https://www.linkedin.com/pulse/insurtech-way-keep-insurance-sector-relevant-matteo-carbone/?trk=mp-reader-card.
5. Carbone, Matteo. "Some secrets they don't want you to know about one of the older InsurTech trends", 7 August 2017, https://www.linkedin.com/pulse/some-secrets-dont-want-you-know-one-older-insurtech-trends-carbone/?trk=mp-reader-card.
6. Carbone, Matteo. "Insurers will still be relevant in the future, even more than yesterday", 9 November 2017, https://www.linkedin.com/pulse/insurers-still-relevant-future-even-more-than-matteo-carbone/?trk=mp-reader-card.
7. Carbone, Matteo. "Five Crazy InsurTech Predictions for 2017", 30 december 2016, http://www.finsmes.com/2016/12/five-crazy-insurtech-predictions-for-2017-by-matteo-carbone.html.
8. Carbone, Matteo. "Insurance Telematics Is Not (Only) UBI." LinkedIn, 21 October 2015 (https://www.linkedin.com/pulse/ insurance-telematics-only-ubi-matteo-carbone/).
9. Carbone, Matteo. "A concrete approach to focus innovation efforts in the insurance sector", 14 July 2016, (https://www.linkedin.com/pulse/my-four-ps-insurtech-matteo-

carbone/?lipi=urn%3Ali%3Apage%3Ad_flagship3_profile_view_base_post_details%3BNxztPKEzR3qH%2Bpuj%2BWU6yw%3D%3D)

10. Carbone, Matteo; Naujoks, Henrik; O'Neill, Sean, "Black Boxes Could Yield Gold in Connected Insurance", 18 September 2016, http://www.bain.com/publications/articles/black-boxes-could-yield-gold-in-connected-insurance.aspx.

11. Carbone, Matteo; Negri, Pietro; Harb, Marco. "Paper Connected and Sustainable Insurance", 20 December 2016, http://www.irsa.it/it/n/paper-connected-and-sustainable-insurance/.

12. Carbone, Matteo. "Motor insurance telematics - Five value creation levers", 1 October 2014, https://www.linkedin.com/pulse/20141001070148-6024099-motor-insurance-telematics-five-value-creation-levers/?trk=mp-reader-card.

13. Carbone, Matteo. "Health insurance - Telematics opportunity", 7 October 2014, https://www.linkedin.com/pulse/20141007053518-6024099-health-insurance-telematics-opportunity/?trk=mp-reader-card.

14. Carbone, Matteo. "Telematics and insurance risk selection", 21 May 2015, https://www.linkedin.com/pulse/telematics-insurance-risk-selection-matteo-carbone/?trk=mp-reader-card.

15. Carbone, Matteo. "Motor telematics – Loss ratio improvement", 7 April 2015, https://www.linkedin.com/pulse/motor-telematics-loss-ratio-improvement-matteo-carbone/?trk=mp-reader-card.

16. Carbone, Matteo. "Technology integration in the health insurance business", 10 December 2014, https://www.linkedin.com/pulse/20141210081320-6024099-technology-integration-in-the-health-insurance-business/?trk=mp-reader-card.

17. Carbone, Matteo. "Individual pricing - Insurance motor telematics approaches", 25 June 2015, https://www.linkedin.com/pulse/individual-pricing-insurance-motor-telematics-matteo-carbone/?trk=mp-reader-card.

18. Carbone, Matteo. "Does Insurance as a Service (IaaS) work October 2015, https://www.linkedin.com/pulse/does-insurance-service-iaas-work-matteo-carbone/?trk=mp-reader-card.
19. Carbone, Matteo. "Connected cars & insurance claims: a new paradigm, made in Italy", 23 November 2015, https://www.linkedin.com/pulse/connected-cars-insuranceclaims-new-paradigm-made-italy-matteo-carbone/?trk=mp-reader-card.
20. Carbone, Matteo. "2016 insurance innovation trends: my predictions", 15 February 2016, https://www.linkedin.com/pulse/2016-insurance-innovation-trends-my-predictions-matteo-carbone/?trk=mp-reader-card.
21. Carbone, Matteo. "My InsurTech mental framework", 16 March 2016, https://www.linkedin.com/pulse/my-insurtech-mental-framework-matteo-carbone/?trk=mp-reader-card.
22. Carbone, Matteo. "Secrets InsurTechs can learn from the auto insurance industry's telematics experience", 20 May 2016, https://www.linkedin.com/pulse/secrets-insurtechs-can-learn-from-auto-insurance-matteo-carbone/?trk=mp-reader-card.
23. Carbone, Matteo. "My four Ps of InsurTech", 14 July 2016, https://www.linkedin.com/pulse/my-four-ps-insurtech-matteo-carbone/?trk=mp-reader-card.
24. Carbone, Matteo. "Connected insurance is here to stay—are you ready for this new insurance paradigm?", 26 September 2016, https://www.linkedin.com/pulse/connected-insurance-here-stayare-you-ready-new-paradigm-carbone/?trk=mp-reader-card.
25. Carbone, Matteo. "The future of insurance is Insurtech", 14 November 2016, https://www.linkedin.com/pulse/future-insurance-insurtech-matteo-carbone/?trk=mp-reader-card.
26. Carbone, Matteo. "Let's do it…if you trust on InsurTech", 25 April 2017, https://www.linkedin.com/pulse/lets-do-itif-you-trust-insurtech-matteo-carbone/?trk=mp-reader-card.

27. Christen, Robert Peck, Richard Rosenberg, and Veena Jayadeva. "Financial Institutions with a 'Double-Bottom Line': Implications for the Future of Microfinanc." *CGAP Occasional Paper*, No. 8, July 2004 (https://www.cgap.org/sites/default/ files/CGAP-Occasional-Paper-Financial-Institutions-with-a- Double-Bottom-Line-Implications-for-the-Future-of-Microfinance-Jul-2004.pdf).
28. Eaton, Kit. "The Future According to Schmidt: 'Augmented Humanity,' Integrated into Google." *Fast Company*, 25 January 2011 (https://www.fastcompany.com/1720703/future-according -schmidt-augmented-humanity-integrated-google).
29. Hans, Joel. "Telematics Looks Worldwide After Conquering Italian Insurance", 3 October 2016, https://www.rtinsights.com/usage-based-insurance-telematics-trends/
30. Kochhar, Rakesh. "A Global Middle Class Is More Promise than Reality." Pew Research Center, 13 August 2015 (http:// www.pewglobal.org/2015/07/08/a-global-middle-class-is-more-promise-than-reality/).
31. Kushmaro, Philip. "The IoT and Big Data: Making the Connection." *Huffington Post*, 24 September 2017 (https://www.huffingtonpost.com/philip-kushmaro/ the-iot-and-big-data-maki_b_12116608.html).
32. Poushter, Jacob. "Smartphone Ownership and Internet Usage Continues to Climb in Emerging Economies." Pew Research Center, 22 February 2016 (http://www. pewglobal.org/2016/02/22/smartphone-ownership-and-internet -usage-continues-to-climb-in-emerging-economies).
33. Shacklett, Mary. "Why Your Company Might Want to Consider Outsourcing Big Data Preparation." TechRepublic, 16 October 2017 (https://www.techrepublic.com/article/why-your-company-might-want-to-consider-outsourcing-big-data-preparation).
34. Silvello, Andrea. "The Three Pillars of Connected Insurance", Harvard Economics Review, 21 April 2016, http://harvardecon.org/?p=3310.

35. Silvello, Andrea. "Connected Health and Its Central Role to Evolution of the Insurance Sector from 'Payer' to 'Player.' " *Journal of Health & Medical Informatics*, Vol. 8, No. 3, Supplement, 2017 (https://www.omicsonline.org/proceedings/connected-health-and-its-central-role-to-evolution-of-the-insurance-sector-from-payer-to-player-68640.html).

36. Silvello, Andrea. "Connected Insurance: Delivering Value with a Customer-Centric Approach" Cutter Business Technology Journal, Vol. 30, No. 9.

37. Silvello, Andrea. "InsurTech Is a Storm Hitting the Old-fashioned Insurance Industry", 7 February 2017, https://www.linkedin.com/pulse/insurtech-storm-hitting-old-fashioned-insurance-andrea-silvello/.

38. Silvello, Andrea. "Push microinsurance is here to capture customers' attention with the right coverage at the right time", 8 May 2017, https://www.linkedin.com/pulse/push-microinsurance-here-capture-customers-attention-right-silvello/.

39. Silvello, Andrea. "The health insurance industry is over passing the traditional 'pay-and-claim' mentality", 16 August 2017, https://www.linkedin.com/pulse/health-insurance-industry-over-passing-traditional-andrea-silvello/?lipi=urn%3Ali%3Apage%3Ad_flagship3_profile_view_base_post_details%3BTwpametKSEyvnSkpRfLWOg%3D%3D.

40. Silvello, Andrea. "Is connected health insurance any good?", 26 July 2017, https://www.linkedin.com/pulse/connected-health-insurance-any-good-andrea-silvello/?lipi=urn%3Ali%3Apage%3Ad_flagship3_profile_view_base_post_details%3BTwpametKSEyvnSkpRfLWOg%3D%3D.

41. Silvello, Andrea. "Microinsurance in developing countries is an Eldorado for Insurtech", 9 June 2017, https://www.linkedin.com/pulse/microinsurance-developing-countries-eldorado-andrea-silvello/?lipi=urn%3Ali%3Apage%3Ad_flagship3_profile_view_base_post_details%3BTwpametKSEyvnSkpRfLWOg%3D%3D.

42. Winnick, Michael. "Putting a Finger on Our Phone Obsession – Mobile Touches: A Study on Humans and Their Tech." dscout, 16 June 2016 (https://blog.dscout.com/mobile-touches).

Report/articles/papers without an author

43. "Data Scientists Spend Most of Their Time Cleaning Data." What's the Big Data? 1 May 2016 (https:// whatsthebigdata.com/2016/05/01/data-scientists-spend-most-of-their-time-cleaning-data).
44. "Get Healthy. Get Rewarded." Discovery Vitality, 2017 (http://www.hr.uct.ac.za/sites/default/files/image_tool/images/236/remuneration/healthcare/discovery/vitality_2017.pdf).
45. "Unveiling the Full Potential of Telematics — How Connected Insurance Brings Value to Insurers and Consumers: An Italian Case Study." Swiss Re, 4 May 2017 (https://www.swissre.com/ library/archive/unveiling_the_full_potential_of_telematics_ how_connected_insurance_brings_value_to_insurers_and_ consumers.html#inline).
46. "Insurance in Developing Countries: Exploring Opportunities in Microinsurance." Lloyd's 360° Risk Insight, Lloyd's/ MicroInsurance Centre (http://www.lloyds.com/~/media/lloyds/ reports/360/360%20other/insuranceindevelopingcountries.pdf).
47. MicroInsurance Centre, LLC (www.microinsurancecentre.org).
48. Venture Scanner, https://www.venturescanner.com/blog/tags/venture%20scanner%20insurtech.
49. IVASS, "Bollettino Statistico Anno IV - N. 12", 10 October 2017, https://www.ivass.it/pubblicazioni-e-statistiche/statistiche/bollettino-statistico/2017/n12/index.html.
50. FT Partners Fintech Industry Research, "Q3 2017 Insurtech Insights", October 2017, https://www.ftpartners.com/docs/FTPartners-3Q17-InsurTechInsights.pdf.

51. "Digital in 2017 Global Overview." Hootsuite, 24 January 2017 (https://www.slideshare.net/wearesocialsg/digital-in-2017- global-overview).
52. "Global Health Workforce Shortage to Reach 12.9 Million in Coming Decades." Press release, World Health Organization, 11 November 2013 (http://www.who.int/mediacentre/news/ releases/2013/health-workforce-shortage/en/).
53. "Unveiling the full potential of telematics", Swiss Re, 4 May 2017, http://www.swissre.com/library/archive/unveiling_the_full_potential_of_telematics_how_connected_insurance_brings_value_to_insurers_and_consumers.html#inline
54. "Insurance Markets: Outlook 2027", Allianz Research, , 5 July 2017, https://www.allianz.com/en/press/news/studies/170705_insurance-markets-outlook-2027/
55. "The Global Fintech Report Q3 2017", CBInsights, 2017, https://www.cbinsights.com/research/report/fintech-trends-q3-2017/.
56. InsurTech Is a Storm Hitting the Old-fashioned Insurance Industry, https://www.linkedin.com/pulse/insurtech-storm-hitting-old-fashioned-insurance-andrea-silvello/.
57. "Changing Role of Advisors in Insurance", Capgemini, 15 September 2017, https://www.capgemini.com/wp-content/uploads/2017/09/changingroleofadvisorsininsuranceweb1504594750.pdf.
58. Telematics is revolutionising insurance through behavioural and contextual analytics, 22 August 2016, https://business-reporter.co.uk/2016/08/22/telematics-revolutionising-insurance-behavioural-contextual-analytics/.
59. "Insuretech is the way to keep the insurance sector relevant", 25 July 2017, https://business-reporter.co.uk/2017/07/25/insuretech-keeps-insurance-sector-relevant/.

I want morebooks!

Buy your books fast and straightforward online - at one of the world's fastest growing online book stores! Environmentally sound due to Print-on-Demand technologies.

Buy your books online at
www.get-morebooks.com

Kaufen Sie Ihre Bücher schnell und unkompliziert online – auf einer der am schnellsten wachsenden Buchhandelsplattformen weltweit!
Dank Print-On-Demand umwelt- und ressourcenschonend produziert.

Bücher schneller online kaufen
www.morebooks.de

OmniScriptum Marketing DEU GmbH
Bahnhofstr. 28
D - 66111 Saarbrücken
Telefax: +49 681 93 81 567-9

info@omniscriptum.com
www.omniscriptum.com

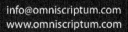

Printed in Great Britain
by Amazon